CLAIRE BRANT

CREDIT REPAIR BIBLE

The Ultimate Guide to Credit Repair, Learn All the
Useful Tips and Best Strategies on How to Repair Your
Credit So You Can Have a Great Financial Future

Descrierea CIP a Bibliotecii Naţionale a României
CLAIRE BRANT
  CREDIT REPAIR BIBLE. The Ultimate Guide to Credit
Repair, Learn All the Useful Tips and Best Strategies on How
to Repair Your Credit So You Can Have a Great Financial
Future / Claire Brant – Bucharest: Editura My Ebook, 2021
  ISBN

CLAIRE BRANT

CREDIT REPAIR BIBLE

The Ultimate Guide to Credit Repair, Learn All the Useful Tips and Best Strategies on How to Repair Your Credit So You Can Have a Great Financial Future

My Ebook Publishing House
Bucharest, 2021

TABLE OF CONTENTS

Introduction 7

What Happened to Your Credit 9

Budgeting 12

   Your Plan of Action 12

Creating a Budget 14

   Making Budget Cuts 16

Managing Your Existing Debt 18

   Refinancing Options 18

Look at your Mortgage Options 20

Building your credit history 22

   Your Credit Report 22

   Understanding Your Credit Score 24

Strategies for credit building 26

Avoiding court 29

   What to do if you receive a summons 30

Collection Agencies 32

Support solutions for low income families 34

Identity theft 35

Re-establish credit after getting a divorce 37

Loan Options 38

    Home Equity Loans 38

    Payday loans 39

    Credit union loans 40

Credit payment plans 42

Cash advances from employers 44

Community emergency assistance plans 46

Small consumer loans 47

Loans from friends and family 49

Filing for Bankruptcy 50

Applying for overdraft protection 52

Tips for Maintaining Your Credit Future 54

    Turn skills and hobbies into cash 54

Maintaining Your Privacy 57

Financial Tips 58

    Looking to the Future 58

    Finances 58

    Around the Home 60

Summary 64

INTRODUCTION

We have put this e book together on Credit Repair and it includes information on debt management, credit repair, time management and other easy solutions for getting yourself out of credit troubles.

We have even included an easy to use Family Budget Planner.

So many people fall into credit trouble each day, and many times through no real fault of their own. This e book is designed to answer all the questions you might have and is intended to answer the most common questions on how to repair your credit. This information is perfect for both individuals as well as families.

This book is intended for anyone dealing with credit and credit issues, including those of you with a bad credit history or no credit at all! By applying the tips within this book you can easily build your credit quickly.

We have even added a helpful section on quick ways to raise money by using your current skills and by cleaning out your home for cash!

Thank you and enjoy reading.

WHAT HAPPENED TO YOUR CREDIT?

The first step to repairing your credit is in understanding what happened and why you are now in financial trouble. Did you lose your job by being laid off? Did you get sick and lost access to your income and have no or very limited health insurance? Or did you overspend and now find yourself with a mess to fix?

All of these have happened to many people in different circumstances. Your first step in fixing your credit is knowing and acknowledging the reasons why your credit situation is the way it is currently. The second step is in knowing how to go about repairing your credit, and yes there is a right and wrong way of doing this!

If you just walk into a credit office and tell them that you can't pay your bill, they automatically assume that you have no money and can't even afford to make one payment. So it is important to know how to approach any type of financial institution.

Basically you want to have all your bills in front of you for the month. Then calculate how much money you have available to pay something on each bill. Prioritize which bills must be paid first. Your mortgage and utilities are high priorities, you don't want to lose having your heat or hydro shut off.

Pay these first and then see what you have left over. If you have a small bill that is just one payment then pay this off next. Then try and make the minimum payments on any other bills you have left.

As soon as you have accomplished this you want to start putting money away for the next month's round of bills.

You need to get yourself into the habit of developing a bill paying strategy. This way you are less likely to default on your bill payments. As soon as you start to miss payments you will begin to have creditors hounding you.

If this is happening to you it might be advisable to think about going to see a credit counsellor. However, that can be another expense for you. If you can be self disciplined and take advice you can take steps to get yourself out of this credit mess that you are currently in.

Self help can be fruitful and by you having to take the steps you are not relying on someone else to fix your problem for you. Self help when done in conjunction with proper education can lead to increased self esteem and confidence. Along with of course, increased financial gain.

BUDGETING

Your Plan of Action

Your first step in helping yourself to repair your credit is to come up with a solid budget. Here you will need to be tight and cut out all excess spending whenever possible.

Look At Your Previous Spending Habits!

Now, before we actually start to create your budget, let's take a look at your spending history. Be honest here and remember you are helping yourself in the end.

Do you consider yourself a quick spender, someone who sees something they like and just buys it? Many of us do this, but it becomes an issue if you do this on a regular basis. As much as credit can be a live saver it can also turn its ugly face on you and become a burden and ruin your life!

If you are an impulse buyer then the next time you feel like purchasing something you need to force yourself to take a step back. Ask yourself why you are considering buying this product. Is it because it is the latest and greatest release of something? Or is it because your appliance broke and you need a new one?

The first reaction would belong to the impulse buyer, while the second is replacing an item because it is broken. Even with this second scenario you want to be careful. Don't replace it unless it is an item which you use everyday like a coffee machine or vacuum cleaner. If it isn't a necessity then put off your purchase for a while. Wait a few weeks and see if you still NEED to buy it! Chances are you have managed without the item and can continue to do so.

If you want to buy the latest product just because all your friends have it, then you will need to put money away and save up for it. By the time you have enough cash saved up you can see whether your desire to own this product is the same. Again chances are that they are not and you have just saved yourself some money. Either put this money aside and use for an emergency fund, or use to pay off a bill.

Whenever you face a situation like this take the time to think it over and congratulate yourself for not making an impulsive buying decision.

CREATING A BUDGET

To start creating a budget you want to get out all of your bills along with your bank statement. You will need to create a worksheet of your income and monthly expenses. This can be done on paper on by using an online software program or an easy to use spreadsheet like the one we have included as a bonus for you.

In one column you want to list your income and in the next all of your expenses. List all of your bills including:

- Mortgage
- Property taxes
- Insurance
- Car Payments
- Student Loan
- Utilities
- Phone bill

- Internet
- Groceries
- Entertainment
- Clothes

List anything and everything that you purchase each month. Then list all sources of income including employment, retirement and interest income.

Make another column for when each payment is due by, allow enough time for the payment to be credited through your bank. Any payments made on a weekend will not be credited until the following Monday.

Then simply go through each amount and deduct the payments from your income and you will either have a positive or negative amount at the end of each month. By listing payment dates you will know if you actually have enough money available at all times of the month to pay your bills.

If budgeting for a month is a little too much for you, then start off by creating a weekly budget and go from there.

This exercise will leave you knowing exactly where you stand financially each month. If you are left will little or no money left over then you must see where you can make some additional cuts.

On the other hand if you have money left over but don't have cash for when the bills are due you must put money aside for future payments. Learn how to save your money, put the extra into your bank account and don't spend it!

* A more detailed Family Monthly Budget is included with this ebook.

Making Budget Cuts

Two of the easiest places to make budget cuts are with entertainment and clothes. If these two sections on your budget are high then this is where you want to look at making budget cuts.

Keep all of your receipts for entertainment and clothes that you purchase for one month. Then divide them into weekly amounts and see what you get. This can be an eye opener for some people. They actually do not realize just how much money they are spending in these categories.

Ask yourself if you really have to eat out as often? Or is it really just a convenience? Be drastic and cut this amount in half and you will be surprised by how much you can save.

Try eating at home more often and going to the movies less often. It is very inexpensive now to order movie channels which offer you a variety of great new movie choices for around $10 a month. You can still have a movie night with your family, just do it at home and make your own snacks. Going to the movies for a family of four can cost around $100 if you include snacks and a drink for each person!

Next take a look at your phone bill. Take a good look at all the extra features and options which you are subscribed to. Do you actually use all of these features?

Many people are making phone calls via the internet with chat features and using their phones to text message. Maybe you can cut down or turn off your long distance calling features, or even your voice mail? With text messages it is almost the same as having a built in answering service. You will open and read the message as soon as you are able to. You may just find that you can live without a lot of these 'extras'.

MANAGING YOUR EXISTING DEBT

Refinancing Options

Many people decide that the easiest way out of debt is to refinance their home or they might even decide to put it up for sale.

If you decide to try and sell your home then look at all the details ahead of time. Make sure you know exactly how much you have left on your mortgage. Then calculate how much money you will have to spend to pay off all of your debts.

Once you have this done you will know exactly how much you have left to use to purchase a new home. Ensure that this will cover your costs and that you can carry over your mortgage if necessary.

You don't want to pay off your mortgage and then apply for a new one, only to be turned down.

Selling your home may be feasible if you own a large home that has increased in value. You might just find that you don't require so much space and downsizing is a good option for you.

When selling your home with the intention of getting top dollar it is worthwhile to make any repairs to your home as necessary. This will avoid a potential buyer coming in with a low offer to offset any repair costs. These repairs can be fixing drafty windows, replacing carpet and installing a new furnace or air conditioner.

To find the current resale value for your home you should speak to a qualified real estate agent. They can advise you on what a fair listing price would be and would you can realistically expect to receive. If you know you stand to make a good profit on your home then selling can be a good solution to repairing your credit.

Don't forget to include additional moving expenses if you go this route. Renting a moving van can be expensive and it can be cheaper to have family and friends help you out.

Also remember that your family will still require somewhere to live, so even if the thought of selling your home to get out of debt but be tempting. It may not always be the best solution.

LOOK AT YOUR MORTGAGE OPTIONS

Before making any drastic decisions over your mortgage take a good look at the terms and conditions of your mortgage. There may be things in your agreement that could be beneficial to you.

It might be possible to change your payment terms or even consolidate another loan onto your mortgage. Many people often put their property tax payments in their mortgage agreement. This is a bad idea as you are then paying un-necessary interest on your taxes. You are better off to have a separate account for your taxes each month. Unless your state allows you to pay your taxes monthly, this helps avoid having to come up with a large monthly payment when your taxes are due.

A good idea is to actually go and speak with your bank manager and see what options, if any are available to you on your mortgage account.

Many mortgages allow you to be late a certain number of times throughout the year without incurring any penalties. Of course you must still make the payment but paying later could be very helpful in certain situations.

If you become sick or injured at work you may have Home Mortgage Insurance in place. This type of insurance agreement will pay your monthly payments for you while sick or injured. Many people are unaware that they have this type of coverage built into their mortgage. It is a great benefit to have and can easily help free up cash in an emergency.

BUILDING YOUR CREDIT HISTORY

Your Credit Report

When attempting to rebuild your credit your first step is to take an in-depth look at your credit report. Your credit report is available to you at no charge once a year from the three major credit bureaus. Each report can in fact be different, this is why it is so important to check all three!

The main thing you want to remember is that the top three companies are in competition with each other. They all want you to subscribe to them and they do not share information.

You are entitled to one free copy each year of your credit report. In addition if your credit application was turned down, you can request another free report. But you must include a copy of the denial with your request. The same applies if you become a victim of identity theft. Send a copy of the police report to the credit bureaus and they will issue you a new report at no charge.

The information found on your credit report will contain your current name, address, date of birth, spouses name, your social insurance number and your current place of employment.

The bulk of the credit report will contain information on your financial status. This includes accounts, loans and when the account was opened, the current balance and the payment history.

You will also have the ability to see who has requested credit checks on you in the last six months. This can include companies who wish to offer you a promotional credit card, and those creditors that are monitoring your account.

Too many credit requests can signal an alert as this looks as though you are suddenly trying to obtain lots of new credit. There is no law to protect you against people looking at your credit history. But you also have the right to contact the companies concerned and ask them the purpose of their credit checks.

There is a section on your credit report entitled Public Record Information and this contains information on tax liens, bankruptcies, foreclosures and possibly any arrests and convictions. Some States are also including information on delinquent child support payments.

Your Credit Report will probably seem incomplete to you and even outdated. This is because the Credit Bureaus rely on the financial institutions to report to them regularly. If they do not, then your credit report will not show current information. Many auto dealers, medical providers and utility companies are guilty of not reporting on time. This inadvertently affects your credit report and credit rating.

Understanding Your Credit Score

Your credit score is based on the FICO rating. This is a system which was developed by Fair, Isaac and Company in 1956. Today software has been developed on this rating system and it is commonly used throughout the United States.

The system uses information from your credit history including the length of your credit history and how long your accounts have been open. They also use information on loans, mortgages and from the public records.

This information is then combined into a three digit score usually from 300 to 950. These numbers are then placed into a category and this determines the quality of your credit status.

Prime – Your score will be above 680 and this allows you to get great interest rates on all your loans, mortgages and credit cards.

Sub Prime – Your score will be below 680 and this results in higher interest rates.

Shafted – Your score is below 560. Even though you may still get loans and credit cards, you will often be asked for security deposits or acquisition fees. Your interest rates are likely to be in the 22% and above range.

Being in the Shafted range will not allow you to get a mortgage and it can also hurt your job applications.

STRATEGIES FOR CREDIT BUILDING

Your best strategies for building good credit are to pay your bills and loans on time. Plus you want to keep your balance as low as possible. High outstanding balances can result in a negative impact on your credit score.

A simple tip is to pay about $5 more than your minimum balance, this will help to build your credit.

You can also apply for a secured credit card. This will require you to make a deposit into a savings account, but is an easy way to start building or rebuilding your credit. Retail credit cards which can only be used at one store are easier to get approved for. But remember that these tend to come with higher interests rates. Have a low limit and purchase small items and then immediately pay them off.

Before applying for a secured credit card check what fees apply. Many of these types of cards have application and even monthly fees built into them. So be careful before making this decision.

If you have unused credit you should use this up before applying for more credit. Unused credit has a high impact on determining your credit score. Try not to use more than 50% of your available balance on any credit card. The higher your balances the higher risk you are determined to be.

Check your credit reports and get any errors and discrepancies fixed. If not removed negative items will stay on your credit report for seven years. Bankruptcies stay on there for 10 years.

When taking out a large loan such as a mortgage you want to take the time and read all the terms and conditions. This way you won't be in for any unexpected surprises. If applying for your first mortgage you may have to have additional insurance coverage for the mortgage itself. Plus there can be additional upfront fees that have to be paid.

Using a good realtor can help you find an affordable home and they have experience in knowing where to find the best mortgages and benefits.

Keeping your accounts open for longer time periods is another key way to build good credit. Even if you don't use the accounts that often, leave it open and open a new account if necessary for other purposes.

When using credit you want to use several types of credit. This not only includes using regular credit cards, but also using credit from retail stores and instalment loans. This shows potential creditors that you understand credit and that you know how to use credit properly.

You must remember too, that even if you pay off a large chunk on your credit card it can still take at least 30 days before an improvement is shown on your credit rating. To help improve your credit rating it really does help to have a credit card from one of the top names, Visa, MasterCard, Discover and American Express.

AVOIDING COURT

Going to court can be really stressful and costly. It is in your best interests to try and avoid this step if at all possible.

The easiest way to avoid being taken to court by your creditors is to prove that you are trying to pay down your debt. It is important to keep records of all your payments no matter how small. This way you have proof that you have been making payments.

By contacting your creditors you are at least making an attempt to get your credit in order. All creditors, lawyers and collection agencies are open to discussions and will listen to any solutions which you may have. They are more than willing to try and come up with a plan of action for you. No one really wants the hassle and aggravation of going through the court system.

Even if you have all ready received a summons you can contact your creditors lawyers. Attempt to pay off the loan if possible or negotiate a payment plan and this can save you from having to go in front of a judge.

What to Do if You Receive a Summons:

If you ignore your summons and don't show up in court you will forfeit your right to argue your case.

The easiest way to reply to a summons is to read it carefully and then respond to it. Most States give you around 20 days to make a response. Your next step is to go to the listed courthouse and fill out a notice of appearance. Fill it out as directed and send copies to those involved as instructed.

You must provide an answer to the summons and as you are the defendant you will need to answer each claim separately. This is where you can disagree with the statements or even state that you do not know if the facts are true.

Once filled out you must file your report and pay any fees as necessary. Doing this step protects your rights to argue the case. You will then appear in court on the correct date and submit any further evidence you have. The judge will then make their ruling.

If you ignore or fail to respond to a summons this allows the creditor to garnish your wages or bank account for the amount owed. If you require legal advice and cannot afford a lawyer then seek the aid of places such as the Salvation Army, the United Way and Legal Aid services.

If a garnishment is approved this can mean that any cheques you write will bounce and that your debit card will be declined. It is definitely a situation that you want to avoid at all costs.

COLLECTION AGENCIES

Collection Agencies have a bad reputation and they can be worse to deal with than your creditor. A collection agency is used by a creditor after all attempts at getting you to pay your debt have failed. They are known as a third party source and represent many different companies.

Collection Agencies take the time and effort to track you down. So if you have moved to avoid your creditors, don't be surprised if the collection agency tracks you down.

Many collection agencies have access to huge databases of information. They will search through phone books and even call friends and family members to track you down. They have even been known to pose as a long lost friend in an attempt to locate a person's whereabouts.

You will find it much easier to deal with your creditor directly than suffer the consequences of a collection agency. If you fear that you are headed in this direction then take the necessary steps to contact your creditor and start negotiations.

Many States have laws in force which restrict the hours that a collection agency can call you. It can also be illegal for them to call your place of employment, unless your employer allows that type of call.

It is also against the law for the collection agency to repeatedly call your home or threaten you into making payments. However, remember you are liable for your debt and must make your payments.

SUPPORT SOLUTIONS
FOR LOW INCOME FAMILIES

Many times Social Services will help you make payments towards your utility bills if you are on a low income. They can also provide you with ways to get extra food for your children by issuing coupons or going to a food bank. This also applies to seniors, you may be entitled to discounts aimed specifically at seniors.

IDENTITY THEFT

Being a victim of identity theft can be extremely difficult to deal with. It can be hard just to prove to anyone who you are. If you become a victim of identity theft you must ask the credit bureaus to place a FREEZE on your account. This signifies that you are a victim.

You will need to prove to the credit bureaus that your identity was stolen. This can be done by filing a police report. Ask for a copy of the report and then make additional copies and send them to the three credit bureaus.

A freeze alert on your credit account is a protection and allows you to still apply for loans and credit cards. If you do not ask for a freeze the credit bureaus put up a Fraud Alert and you will never be approved for credit!

Always monitor all of your accounts to ensure that no more strange activity is taking place. You will need to inform your utility and Phone Company plus your credit card company of your identity theft. Get them to freeze your old cards and accounts and open up new ones for you.

Don't forget about your social insurance number and driver's license. Inform the appropriate offices. They should be able to tell you if your numbers have been used recently and for what purpose.

RE-ESTABLISH CREDIT
AFTER GETTING A DIVORCE

If you previously had no credit in your name now is the time to build your credit. If you were both listed on your loans and utility bills you must now set up accounts in your name only. Be sure to cancel all joint accounts and check your credit report to ensure it reflects this change.

You can also rebuild credit with a credit card, but watch out for interest rates. Especially those companies that offer interest free periods that suddenly turn into higher than normal interest rates.

You want to establish a low balance on your credit card and then pay it off. Do this several times to improve your credit history.

Moving several times in a year makes creditors question your credit history and is cause for attention. It can be difficult to not have to move after a divorce. But try to stay at the same address for at least one year if possible.

LOAN OPTIONS

Home Equity Loans

Many people look to getting a home equity loan as a way of getting themselves out of debt. Unfortunately most financial institutions will only give you a home equity loan if your credit is in good standing.

With a home equity loan you are basically borrowing money against the value of your home. This is also known as a second mortgage and they are normally given out for a shorter time period than the traditional mortgage. In some parts of the United States it is possible to deduct the interest on a home equity loan on your income taxes.

There is a difference between a home equity loan and a home equity line of credit. A line of credit is a revolving line of funds available to you. A home equity loan is a onetime loan with a fixed interest rate. The interest rate on a line of credit is normally based on Prime rate plus a margin factor.

Applying for a home equity loan can actually get you deeper into debt, and it is not advisable to go this path at all. There are many other fees associated with a home equity loan and these can include:

- Appraisal fees
- Originator fees
- Title fees
- Stamp duties
- Arrangement fees
- Closing fees
- Early pay-off fee

With a home equity loan you need to consult with a professional who can advise you on all the terms and conditions associated with this type of loan. Too many people take a home equity loan without understanding the full implications. Then when they cannot repay this loan they are in fear of losing their home.

Payday Loans

Payday loans are often referred to as a pay check advance. They are a short term loan that is intended to carry you over until your next pay day. Or this is what they were meant to do.

Today many people are using payday loans as a means to reducing their debt and paying their monthly bills. The terms and conditions for using payday loans are different in all counties. Even within the United States each state has its own rules pertaining to payday loans.

To apply for a payday loan you will normally be required to provide proof of employment, or at least a bank statement. Depending upon your location and which financial institution you wish to use this may or may not be required.

Your payday loan will have a maturity date and you will be required to pay back your loan with interest by this date. If you fail to do so, then additional charges will be added and this can become quite significant.

Taking a payday loan can turn into a huge expense and you do have other options.

Credit Union Loans

Credit unions work in a similar way as banks but they do have several differences. Credit Unions are actually non profit organizations but that is not to say they are a charity. The main goal of a credit union is to offer service over aiming to make a profit.

The Credit Union is run by a board of members who are elected volunteers. These board members run the union and help make all the decisions.

Credit Unions will usually offer fewer services than the regular banks. They focus on providing services which they know their customers will need. Because of this Credit

Unions are actually known to provide good competition for the larger banks. Once you have established a good relationship with a Credit Union you can normally receive excellent rates from them.

Credit Unions normally loan money to small business at good rates. This is why many people choose to use them for business start ups. Some Credit Unions do offer loans for personal use and you will have to check with your local unions to find out all the details.

If they do this can be a good way to manage your debt simply because of the rates that they offer to customers.

CREDIT PAYMENT PLANS

It is possible to negotiate a credit payment plans with your credit card company or loan company. A good way to achieve this is by approaching the company telling them that you want to clean up your credit report. In this way you are asking for their help, and this normally goes over better.

By setting up a payment plan the credit knows that they will receive the money and will be happy to remove the item from the credit report for you. Sometimes all it takes is asking the right way to get something done easily!

When negotiating with the credit company tell them what you ARE able to manage each month. Don't make excuses for anything and don't tell them what you CAN'T do! This means making a budget before hand so you don't miss any payments.

Most companies are more than happy to settle for less than full price and some will even drop down to 70% for a payment plan.

If you have more than one creditor start off making a payment plan with the lowest amount first. This way it can be cleared from your credit report quickly. Then move onto the next, leaving the highest for last.

Make sure you get all settlement agreements in writing and keep additional copies of each. If you receive phone calls take down the caller's name, the date and time of the call along with relevant details of what was discussed.

When approaching any loan company always be polite. They are so used to dealing with angry and frustrated people that a polite person will throw them off. They will be more responsive and open to your suggestions.

If your company refuses to negotiate any type of credit payment plan, then wait a few months before approaching them again. In the meantime try and make some type of payment so that they can see that you are trying to pay down your debt.

CASH ADVANCES FROM EMPLOYERS

Getting a cash advance from your employer can be difficult. Some companies have no issues with helping out an employee in an emergency. But it is doubtful if they will enter into a long term cash advance with you.

Requesting a cash advance from your employer should only be done if first you know they offer this and second if it truly is an unplanned emergency.

An alternative option is to apply for a payday loan. Plus this way your employer won't know that you have had an emergency. Payday loans operate in the same way as a short term loan which is paid back when you receive your next pay check.

COMMUNITY EMERGENCY ASSISTANCE PLANS

To get help through a community emergency assistance plan you have to register and meet certain criteria. Depending upon which program you apply to your assistance amount may be limited. Some States only offer assistance plans at certain times of the year.

Most community emergency assistance plans (CEAP) are in place to educate you and help you manage your finances better. They are not there to get you out of financial trouble with cold hard cash.

These types of plans are aimed at seniors who are trying to keep their dignity while maintaining their current lifestyle. They offer advice in regards to services such as meals on wheels and transportation services.

Each County normally has resources available for you through their program. These resources will provide you with details on how to obtain help for paying your rent or utility bill.

Contacting a CEAP can act as a lifeline and put you in touch with someone who can help you deal with your emergency. You should never be afraid or ashamed to ask for assistance if you truly need it.

SMALL CONSUMER LOANS

Small consumer loans are short term loans which don't require any security. This means you don't have to pledge your house or other assets in order to be approved for the loan. This type of loan is helpful for an unexpected emergency or to help tide you over until pay day.

This is a good option if you have a few small bills that can be paid off by taking one larger loan. This is great for keeping your utility bills and phone bills up to date. You could also use a small consumer loan to pay off a small balance on your credit card.

Many small loans can be applied for online and do not require a credit check. With fast approval times you could easily have access to funds within 24 – 48 hours.

Another very good use of taking a small consumer loan is that it is an excellent way to build up your credit rating. As most small loans are for around $1,500 you can pay back the amount quickly and gain points for your credit report.

The rates on small loans may be better for purchasing items such as a new washer and dryer or even a used car. It is worth checking into these types of loans before paying higher interest rates from other financial institutions.

LOANS FROM FRIENDS AND FAMILY

Asking for a loan from a good friend or family member is another possible way to help you pay off your debts. Of course this will depend upon your relationship with your family and the circumstances.

Most families are only too willing to help each other out if you find yourself in an unexpected situation. Maybe someone in the family is off work due to illness or you might find yourself suddenly without a job.

If you do end up getting a loan from a family member or friend then be sure to write up all the details of the loan on paper. Include the amount loaned, the interest rate if any and the scheduled payment plan. It is a wise idea to record each payment made and for both parties to have a receipt. This way there can be no complaints or issues down the road!

Before accepting a loan from a family member, be sure that they can afford to lend you the money. You don't want to run the risk of them getting into financial trouble because they helped you out.

FILING FOR BANKRUPTCY

Many people think that filing for bankruptcy is the easiest thing to do. For some this can be a huge mistake and end up causing more problems than it solves. Filing for Bankruptcy is not something that should be taken lightly. You want to explore all your other options first.

Consulting with a bankruptcy expert is your best choice if you are considering this option. A bankruptcy can easily stay on your financial records for up to 10 years. The Bankruptcy Abuse Prevention and Consumer Protection Act ("BAPCPA") was amended in October of 2005 and now states that a person must seek financial advice for credit before filing for bankruptcy.

Going for credit counselling beforehand is hopefully a way that you can discover different ways to get out of debt and avoid bankruptcy.

It is possible to file for bankruptcy without a lawyer but unless you know what you are doing it is not recommended. The fees for filing bankruptcy will vary and you need to choose a lawyer which can handle your case and that you can afford.

There are some places which will file your bankruptcy for you for free. Some lawyers will take payment afterwards or in instalments.

Once you have started the process then any correspondence you receive from your credit card company and other loan institutions should be forwarded to your lawyer. There is something called an automatic stay in place and this prevents any creditors from contacting you.

One very important note is that once your bankruptcy proceedings have started then you must NOT use your credit cards anymore. If you continue to use your credit cards the credit company can challenge your discharge. Accumulating debt knowing you cannot repay it can void your discharge as well.

Your employer and landlord will not be notified of your bankruptcy but your record is made public. So anyone that wants to could find out that you have started bankruptcy proceedings. If a new employer or landlord does a credit check they will see that you have filed for bankruptcy and this could harm you.

Make sure that you keep all your documents pertaining to your bankruptcy for at least a year if not more.

APPLYING FOR OVERDRAFT PROTECTION

Having overdraft protection on your bank account can be a very useful thing to have. This protection will allow any of your monthly bills such as your mortgage to be paid even though you may not have sufficient funds in your account.

However, the bank will only pay this amount if they have agreed to issue you overdraft protection. If your bank account becomes overdrawn without this agreement you may be subject to interest fees and other additional charges.

Your overdraft agreement with your bank will cover you up to a certain dollar amount. This agreement normally covers withdrawals done at an ATM machine, debit card, checks and electronic transfers.

If you have no overdraft protection then your checks would be bounced and returned to you as unpaid.

You also have the option of applying for an overdraft line of credit. This is done by filling out an application form and waiting for approval. Your line of credit is considered a loan and interest charges will apply as normal.

If you have a checking account, a savings account and a line of credit you can get these accounts linked together. Then if there was not enough money in one account the money would be withdrawn from one of the other accounts.

TIPS FOR MAINTAINING
YOUR CREDIT FUTURE

Turn skills and hobbies into cash

When you need money fast take a look at what skills you have. Are you handy around the house, do you enjoy gardening or animals? You could offer a pet walking service in your area. Or how about fixing up decks and gardens in the summer months?

Another great service to offer is to go grocery shopping for seniors. Building garden sheds and planter boxes is yet another idea.

Don't forget about having a Yard Sale too. Clean out your house including the basement and garage and put all your unused belongings into a sale. You can advertise your yard sale on Craig's List and any other local websites.

If you are desperate for money and have valuables such as jewellery, antiques or electronics these could be sold at antique stores or pawn shops. Though this is really only advisable in extreme circumstances.

Car washes and offering detailing such as cleaning the inside of vehicles is a good way to earn some extra cash. You could visit local businesses and offer to clean employee's cars on the inside while they work.

If you enjoy baking why not hold a bake sale alongside your yard sale? Muffins, cookies and a cold drink are sure to go over well with your visitors and can bring in much needed additional cash.

Make money by collecting scrap metal and selling it. Even picking up larger garbage items around your neighbourhood is easy and profitable to do. Especially if you own a pickup truck or trailer!

It is possible to raise money by participating in research studies and selling your plasma.

For those who enjoy crafts then making and selling small crafts is perfect. You can even target local businesses and offer to make them items with their company name on it.

If you own a larger home then you could consider renting out a room to raise extra money. If the room is private and has a separate entrance or kitchen you can charge more each month. This is a great option if you live in an area with a local college or university.

If all the above fail then your last recourse would be to try and find another temporary job to get you through your cash flow situation. It may be difficult to fit in two jobs but it might be a better solution than going deeper into debt, or losing your home.

Finding a temporary job can be a good choice at Christmas time when many stores require additional help for a few weeks. Other choices include landscape companies and golf courses during the summer months. If you enjoy golf you can earn money and probably get some free rounds of golf at the same time!

MAINTAINING YOUR PRIVACY

The easiest way to maintain your privacy in regards to your financial status is to avoid using credit as much as possible. This means paying with cash whenever possible. You should also avoid giving out your driver's license number too. If a retailer asks for your telephone number or address, you have the right to refuse. There is no law stating that you must give out this information.

If participating in an online or phone survey limit the amount of information which you give out. Never give out your social insurance number and driver's license information. This can be used to look into your credit history and more.

Even when filling out warranty information try to limit the amount of personal information which you provide. Only fill out what is absolutely necessary.

FINANCIAL TIPS

Looking to the Future

Once you finally have your finances under control and your debt paid off you can start looking forward to a positive future. Now that you have freed up some money you want to look at opening some type of retirement fund.

Finances

You want to make it a priority to add money to this fund each month. Many banks and financial institutions can easily help you set up a direct payment method each month. This monthly solution often works better for most people. Trying to come up with a large payment just before tax deadline time can be very difficult.

Another great tip for paying down your mortgage is to switch to weekly payments. This can really reduce the number of years you will carry your mortgage. Many banks allow you to make extra payments without penalties at least once a year. Try using your income tax return or bonus to pay off your mortgage faster!

Many employers offer stock options and 401k choices. They will often match dollar for dollar your contributions each pay period. This can be a great way to really build up a good retirement income. If this is offered by your employer you should really try and take advantage of it.

As you look to the future you want to remember not to get into the habit of overspending again. Always try to shop for bargains and really think about buying something new.

Avoid impulse shopping and save enough cash to pay for the new item upfront.

You should look at your bank account options and see if there is a better account with cheaper options. If you find you use your debit card so many times a month, you might wish to opt for an account that has additional debit transactions per month. Enquire at your bank for your best options.

Around the Home

Take a look at your house, car and other insurances and see if you can get a better deal. Many times having all your policies with one company will get you a nice discount.

Use coupons, you may have seen many TV's shows on coupon shopping. You don't have to go to the extreme but it is possible to save a good deal of money each month when using coupons. No matter what you are purchasing look online to see if any discounts or special offers are being offered.

If you still want to enjoy going to the movies with your family try going to a matinee showing instead. This can cut your costs in half. Or you could arrange a great family movie night at home instead. This would decrease the cost of snacks and each family member could prepare their own snack for the movie. This way you can easily afford to rent more than one movie by watching at home.

Vacations – of course you still want to travel with your family, to reduce the cost try to go in an off season. The prices are much cheaper and this won't strain your budget as much. If you can book your trip just as peak season turns into off season.

The weather will probably be the same and your savings will be substantial.

If you currently rent your home and lease your car look at what it would cost to actually own these items instead. Sometimes the costs and benefits of owning your car or home are much better than renting. By owning your home your mortgage payments become an investment in your future. If property values increase then you will have made a wise investment in yourself and possibly something to pass onto your children.

Maintaining your home and car will end up saving you lots of money. Each year look around your home and fix leaky taps, drafty windows and doors that don't fit properly. Small repairs are much easier to fix than waiting until something major happens and you require a repair that could cost thousands of dollars.

The same applies to your homes insulation, make sure doors, fireplaces and windows are well insulated. This can really earn you huge savings on your hydro bill.

Close your heating vents in rooms that you don't use. If you have a spare bedroom or your child is off at college, why heat that space. The same goes for the basement, turning off a couple of vents can save you lots of money, especially if you don't use your basement that much.

It is worth it to stock up on everyday items when they are offered at a discount. Things like paper towels, shower gels and shampoos will keep well for months and can save you tons of money.

Plan your shopping trips so you can do all your errands at one time. Try to avoid having to run back to the store for small items each day. Unless of course you can easily walk to the store!

See if you can set up a car pool to get your kids to work and even for you to get to work. Maybe there are some other employees that live in the same area. Try to take turns driving each week. This can save you money on gas and delay car repairs.

Shopping online is very popular and another good way to save money. By shopping this way you can save gas money on having to drive long distances to your nearest mall.

You will most likely find great deals and many times large retailers have free or very low shipping costs. Delivery is fast and your item could be received within a couple of days.

Remember if you use your credit card to pay for online purchases you want to pay them off as soon as possible. You don't have to wait for the bill to arrive either. Simply make an extra payment ahead of time, reducing your risk of paying unnecessary interest charges.

If you own a lot of slightly used clothing or even furniture make use of consignment shops. Consignment stores are always looking for great quality items and this allows you to get paid instead of throwing away good clothes.

Always get into the habit of checking your receipts and bank statements. Errors are often made and you might be surprised at just how often you will find a discrepancy.

If your appliance or couch needs replacing consider the cost of having these items repaired first. Sometimes having a couch re-upholstered can be cheaper than buying a brand new one.

If you are accustomed to spending more money at Christmas and vacation time then set up two special accounts. Then during the year you can fund these accounts gradually.

When it comes time to use the money, presto! You have money all ready saved up.

If you keep this above tips in mind all the time you will easily be able to get and keep your finances on track.

SUMMARY

By using the information provided in this ebook you should have enough resources to start getting your finances back on the right track. They say that you can form lasting habits in as little as three weeks. So by budgeting and watching where you spend your money you will quickly feel as though you are developing new habits.

It will take time to get yourself out of debt but the effort you take now will definitely allow you to look towards a good future. By investing in yourself now you can reap the rewards for yourself and your family.

Printed by Libri Plureos GmbH in Hamburg,
Germany